D1545094

WITHDRAWN

BIRTHDAYS OF FREEDOM

BOOK II

Birthdays of
FREEDOM

FROM THE FALL OF ROME
TO JULY 4, 1776

BOOK TWO

GENEVIEVE FOSTER

STATE LIBRARY
REGIONAL CENTER
BOOKMOBILE
CALDWELL, OHIO

THE STATE LIBRARY
65 S. FRONT ST.
COLUMBUS 15, OHIO

CHARLES SCRIBNER'S SONS NEW YORK

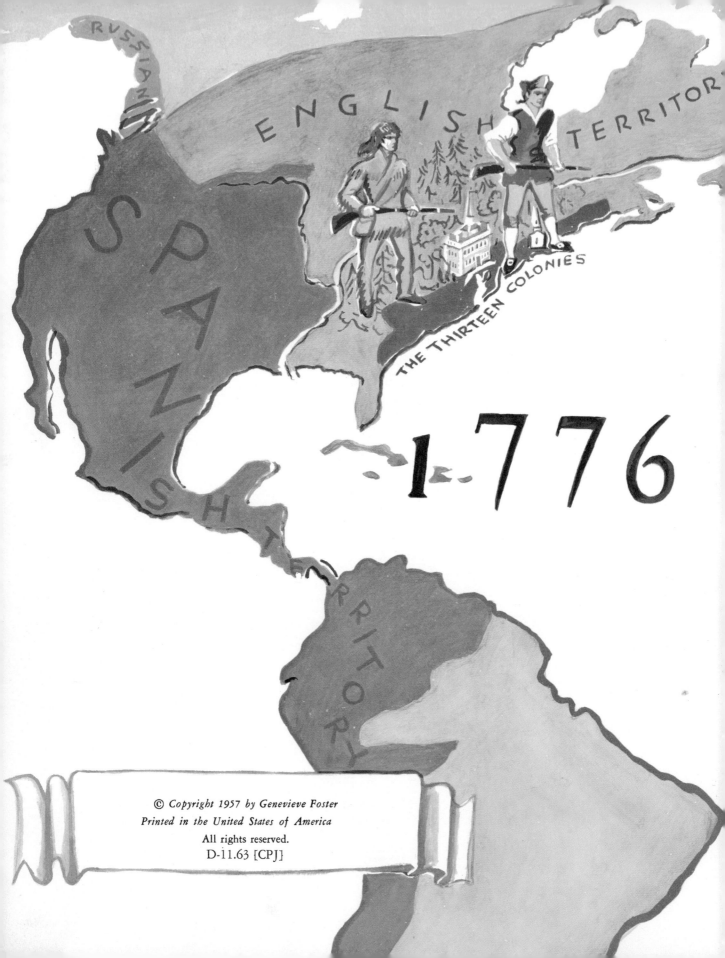

© Copyright 1957 by Genevieve Foster

Printed in the United States of America

All rights reserved.

D-11.63 [CPJ]

B75916

ENGLAND

IN CONGRESS JULY 4, 1776

The unanimous Declaration of the thirteen united States of America

In 1776, just 1300 years after the Fall of Rome, the Liberty Bell was ringing in Philadelphia.

A declaration of independence had been signed. Thirteen American colonies announced to the world that they no longer belonged to the King of England. They had broken away from the mother country to form a new nation known as the United States of America. This was something new in the history of the world. In the old lands of Europe and Asia where savage man first became civilized, nations had grown gradually through the centuries. Here on this new land, where they could start afresh, civilized people had created a nation with the stroke of a pen!

It had taken courage for the men of those thirteen colonies to break the ties that bound them to England, which they still spoke of as "home." It had taken courage to defy the King, to whom they had been trained as children to pledge their allegiance. Only when there seemed no other way to preserve their rights as Englishmen, did those men of the colonies decide to make the break. One of the rights for which they had protested for many years before declaring their independence was the right to tax themselves.

"No freeman, according to the laws of England, should be made to pay a tax to which he has not given his consent." So said John Adams in a Town Meeting held in Boston, Massachusetts, more than ten years before he signed the Declaration. The year was 1765. The tax known as the Stamp Act was arousing indignation in all the colonies from Massachusetts to Georgia.

Down in Williamsburg, Virginia, there was sharp excitement one May morning in the House of Burgesses when Patrick Henry, a back country lawyer, rose to his full height, shambled forward past the green felt-covered table and began to speak. George Washington was there in his seat as a delegate from his county. Thomas Jefferson, a sandy-haired young student with an armful of law books, stood listening in the doorway.

"According to the rights of Englishmen," began Patrick Henry, "the people of Virginia are not obliged to obey the Stamp Act." He recalled other rulers in history who like George III had been too eager for power. "Caesar," he cried, "had his Brutus. Charles I, his Cromwell, and George III . . ."

"Treason!" shouted the chairman of the meeting for, as everyone knew, Julius Caesar had been murdered by Roman senators, and Charles I, King of England, had been beheaded by order of Parliament as "a lesson to all tyrants."

"And George III," continued the speaker, "may well profit by their example."

George III failed to profit. For his example he chose the King of France, the King of Spain, and other absolute monarchs whose dissatisfied people dared not speak up. Yet in America, George III's still loyal and unsuspecting subjects continued to appeal to him for sympathy, and to lay blame for their miserable taxes on the English Parliament.

In 1765, Mr. Benjamin Franklin, from Pennsylvania, was in England on business for that colony. He was summoned to appear in Parliament, before the House of Commons, to answer questions as to what might happen in America if the Stamp Act should not be repealed. His straightforward answer was:

"A total loss of respect the people of America bear to this country."

The former Prime Minister, William Pitt, also asked Benjamin Franklin to call upon him, and came to the point at once with this direct question.

"Does America wish to be independent?"

"No," said Benjamin Franklin. It was not independence, but only their rights as Englishmen that the people of America wanted.

The great Englishman nodded. "When two countries are connected, like England and her colonies," he said, "the greater must necessarily rule, but so rule as not to contradict any rights that belong to both."

Those are the words of William Pitt, England's wise Prime Minister, whose genius had built the British Empire, the first one after 1300 years to resemble the great Roman Empire. In those words William Pitt expressed the golden balance of give and take upon which freedom depends. If those wise words had been heeded, the history of America might have continued to be part of the story of England. Assured of their rights, the men of the colonies might not then have declared their independence.

What were those rights which they talked so much about and valued so highly? Those rights of Englishmen? How did they differ from the rights of Frenchmen or Spaniards? Why? How had these rights been won? What were the beliefs and customs which the first English settlers brought with them to the new world? What, in short, was the heritage of freedom which caused those forefathers to cut themselves off from the old world and start a new nation dedicated to keeping that heritage alive?

The answers are to be found in the long story of England. That takes us back to the last years of the Roman Empire, when German tribes from the North rushed in to destroy the Empire, and give the old Roman colony of Britannia, the new name of England.

What is freedom? German barbarians

About the year 400 the German invasions into the Roman Empire began. First came the Goths, followed by other and fiercer tribes from the northern forests. Breaking the barrier along the Rhine and Danube, they went sweeping down into Italy, into Gaul, into Spain and across the water into Britain, plundering, destroying in clumsy ignorance, then setting up their own rude kingdoms in the broken colonies. And the Roman empire was gone, its law and order destroyed. Roman citizens, once so proud of their freedom, were no longer free, for to be protected by that great system of law and order was what freedom meant to a Roman.

But to a German from the wilderness—that was not freedom. A German was free because he could protect himself. He was an independent warrior. He belonged to no great state. No one gave him orders except a chief of his own choosing. As for the laws governing his tribe . . .

> "On affairs of smaller moment the chiefs consult; on those of greater importance, the whole community. They assemble on stated days, either at the new or full moon . . . they sit armed. Then the King, the chief, and others of importance are heard. If a proposal displease the assembly, they reject it by a grumbling murmur. If it prove agreeable, they clash their javelins, for the most honorable expression of approval is the clash of arms."

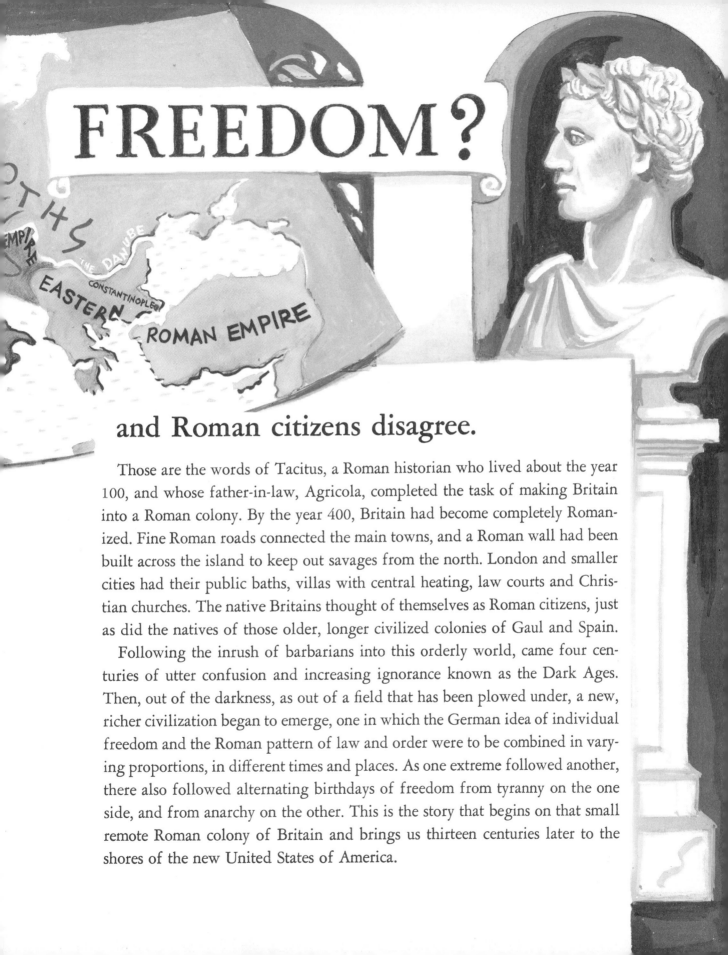

FREEDOM?

and Roman citizens disagree.

Those are the words of Tacitus, a Roman historian who lived about the year 100, and whose father-in-law, Agricola, completed the task of making Britain into a Roman colony. By the year 400, Britain had become completely Romanized. Fine Roman roads connected the main towns, and a Roman wall had been built across the island to keep out savages from the north. London and smaller cities had their public baths, villas with central heating, law courts and Christian churches. The native Britains thought of themselves as Roman citizens, just as did the natives of those older, longer civilized colonies of Gaul and Spain.

Following the inrush of barbarians into this orderly world, came four centuries of utter confusion and increasing ignorance known as the Dark Ages. Then, out of the darkness, as out of a field that has been plowed under, a new, richer civilization began to emerge, one in which the German idea of individual freedom and the Roman pattern of law and order were to be combined in varying proportions, in different times and places. As one extreme followed another, there also followed alternating birthdays of freedom from tyranny on the one side, and from anarchy on the other. This is the story that begins on that small remote Roman colony of Britain and brings us thirteen centuries later to the shores of the new United States of America.

FRIGG WODEN TIW

The Anglo-Saxons invade Britain.

ANGLO SAXON

The poor Roman-Britons on their small remote island! They were deserted when the invasions into Italy began. The Roman soldiers had to be called in to guard Rome. The Britons, unprotected, left to shift for themselves, were easy prey for the wild Picts and Scots from the North who came swarming down upon them. In despair they cried for help to a savage tribe of German sea rovers, called Jutes. Three shiploads of Jutes, warriors with long spears, answered the cry. They jumped to land on the seacoast of Kent, did their fighting, then settled down in Kent and refused to leave. After the Jutes, came the Saxons, more land-hungry German pirates from across the water. What the Saxons took became west, east and south Saxon—or Wes-sex, Essex and Sussex. After the Saxons, came the Angles, the entire tribe, who spread in such numbers over the land that eventually it all came to be called Angle-land, or England. Soon, except for roads and walls, almost every trace of Roman life in Britain had vanished. Britain had become an Anglo-Saxon land, with the old German customs brought from the homeland. There was the general assembly, or "moot," in which every freeman had a voice, and the Witenagemot, or small assembly of wise men, who chose the king and gave him counsel. And over all were the old gods of War, Sky, Thunderbolts and Spring, whose names still remain in four days of our week—Tiw, Woden, Thor and Frigg.

Gaul is invaded by the Franks.

In northwest Gaul, across the Rhine from the Saxon's homeland, was another German tribe who, proud of never being conquered by the Romans, called themselves Franks—or freemen. As a sign of their freedom they never cut their long blond hair.

In 481 these proud Franks lifted on their shields and hailed as king a clever, ferocious young fighter of fifteen by the name of Clovis. Five years later, young Clovis, brandishing his battleax, his blond hair tied in a flying pony tail, calling on Thor and Woden for help, led his pagan warriors to battle and conquered all of northern Gaul.

Then the bishops prayed for the pagan Clovis, and the monks prayed, and his pious wife Clotilda, and St. Genevieve of Paris, who had known his father, all prayed that Clovis should become a Christian. And Clovis did in his own way. He bargained with the God of the Christians before another battle and in return for the victory went to Rheims and was baptized by the bishop. And for good measure added 3000 of his warriors as converts.

Then this "Most Christian King," as he was named by the Pope in Rome, this newly converted Clovis, conquered almost all the rest of Gaul, murdered all possible rivals, and made his the first family of kings in this new kingdom of the Franks, which was to become France.

Church

Pope Gregory I brings the law and order of the Church into an age of confusion.

All Italy was in a panic when, in 590, Pope Gregory I became head of the church in Rome. The Lombards, last and most fearful of the German invaders, were pushing their way down into the peninsula and might have captured Rome itself if Pope Gregory had not been there to take control. There was no one else. The Emperor of the East in Constantinople was too far away; his officers in Italy were too weak. The Pope had to step in. And so the church, in time of need, provided law and order. Pope Gregory commanded generals, provided munitions, and appointed his bishops to govern the cities. From then on, more and more through the Dark Ages, the disorderly world was to be held together —and governed by—the church.

Gregory I had been a monk before he became Pope. After his wealthy father died, he turned his palace home into a monastery, and spent his fortune founding seven others. Through the Dark Ages, monasteries stood like small islands of light in a sea of ignorance. There the monks preserved whatever books had not been destroyed, and kept the skill of writing and the ancient Latin language alive. It was while he was still a monk that Gregory first heard about the Angles and thought of converting them.

and Monastery

In 597

he sent a missionary to England.

This is the story as it was written in Latin, 100 years later by an Anglo-Saxon monk and priest known as the Venerable Bede.

One day, while Gregory was still a monk, he had seen boys from England being sold as slaves in the Roman market place . . .

"Struck by the beauty of their white skin and fair hair he asked from what country or nation they came and was told from the island of Britain. He asked whether these islanders were Christians and was informed that they were pagans. Then, fetching a sigh from the bottom of his heart, he said, 'Alas what a pity that men so fair of face should be devoid of inward grace.' He again asked for the name of the nation and was told that they were called Angles. 'Right' said he, 'for they have angel faces and should be co-heirs with the angels of Heaven.' Then repairing to the bishop of Rome, he entreated him to send some minister into Britain, that it might be converted."

It was not, however, until seven years after Gregory himself became Pope that St. Augustine was sent as a missionary to Britain—to convert King Ethelbert, the King of Kent.

"On the east coast of Kent is the isle of Thanet. Here in this isle landed the servant of our Lord, Augustine, and his companions, being as reported nearly forty men. They had by order of the blessed Pope Gregory taken interpreters of the Franks, and sending to King Ethelbert, signified that they were come from Rome with a joyful message. Some days later the king came to the island and sitting in the open air, ordered Augustine and his companions brought into his presence . . . not in any house, lest according to ancient superstition, if they practiced magical arts they might get the better of him. But they came furnished with divine, not with magic virtue, bearing a silver cross for their banner and the image of our Lord and Saviour painted on a board. The king permitted them to reside in the city of Canterbury, and being converted to the faith let them preach openly and build or repair churches in all places."

Mohammed gives a new religion to the Arabs.

Pope Gregory was thirty, about to become a monk, when the prophet Mohammed was born in Arabia, in Mecca. To this city of crowded bazaars and countless idols, tribesmen from the desert came yearly to buy and sell, and especially to visit a small black stone, the sacred Kaaba.

Until he was forty, Mohammed was a merchant, traveling by camel caravan along the Red Sea on to Jerusalem and Damascus, learning the beliefs of both the Jews and Christians, often praying alone in the desert for understanding. Then, one day, there in the sandy wind, came a voice giving to him the Truth that he must preach: ISLAM—submission to the will of Allah—Allah being the Arab word for the one and only God, creator of mankind. "They who set their faces with resignation toward God, and do what is right—no fear shall come to them, neither shall they be grieved." Those were the words of Mohammed, and this he taught. "Say ye; We believe in God, and in that which was given to the prophets from their Lord—to Abraham, to Moses and to Jesus. No difference do we make between them." There was but one God—one Allah.

So spoke Mohammed, denouncing the many tribal gods and the worship of idols, and so alarming the priestly guardians of the Kaaba, and endangering their business, that they damned him as a madman and drove him from the city. In the year 622, Mohammed and his few poor converts fled from Mecca.

That was the turning point—the Hegira, or Flight of the Prophet. In the next and last ten years of his life, Mohammed became a warrior. He conquered, converted and enlisted the tribes of the desert, and by the sword and the word made himself master of all Arabia, its "prophet, priest and king."

ámmeð

Mediterranean

· Damascus

· Jerusalem

Arabia

· Medina
· Mecca

Old monk recognizes Mohammed as the prophet.

فقال الغوابني فقال النبي ان لايكون له اب ليكون والد فقد خرج ويكون

711 Arabic

Spain, the oldest of the Roman colonies, had been ruled by the Goths for 300 years when, in 711, it was conquered by the Arabs, and with little difficulty. In fact, they came by invitation of a Spanish count who was at outs with the Gothic king. The Arab governor of North Africa, accepting the invitation, shipped troops at once across the narrow strait to the old "Pillar of Hercules" on the other side. The great rock thereafter became known as Gibraltar (*gibal-al Tarik*) meaning the mountain of Tarik, for Tarik was the general, who within a few short months made Spain part of the Empire of Islam. Who was there to stop him? Not the Goths. Their resistance crumbled to pieces after one sharp battle. Not the Spaniards, no less willing to pay taxes to one overlord than to another. Not the Jews who welcomed the more tolerant Moslems. So on went the Arabs, on through Spain to its farthest border. Then, to the alarm of all Christendom, in 732, they crossed the border into France.

Was there no stopping them?—these Moors, these Moslems, these Saracens—these infidels? Were all Christians to lose their freedom?

No. At Tours, the Arab horsemen with their curved swords and flying turbans struck a wall of iron—a human wall of mailed warriors—Franks, commanded by one known as Charles the Hammer. Fear of the Arabs had made the Frankish chieftains stop fighting each other and unite against the enemy.

The Arabs retired into Spain, and made of Spain the most enlightened spot in Europe during the rest of the Dark Ages. In the old, long civilized lands of the East, which the Arab empire included, there had been no blackout of culture. All the ancient learning which the Arabs found there they carried into Spain, where they established universities at Cordova, Toledo,

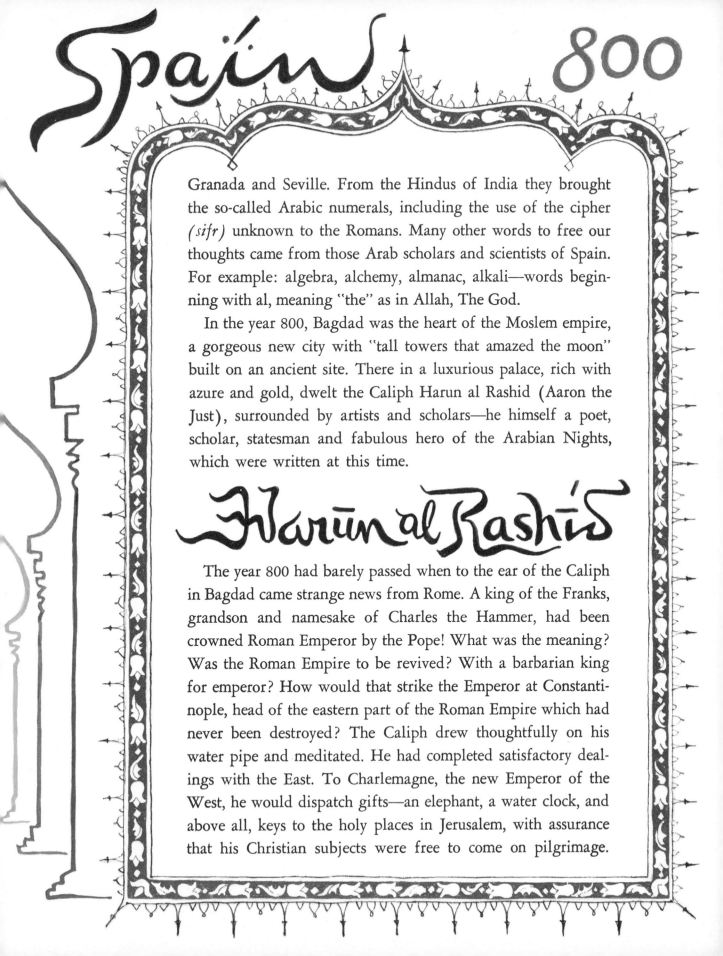

Granada and Seville. From the Hindus of India they brought the so-called Arabic numerals, including the use of the cipher *(sifr)* unknown to the Romans. Many other words to free our thoughts came from those Arab scholars and scientists of Spain. For example: algebra, alchemy, almanac, alkali—words beginning with al, meaning "the" as in Allah, The God.

In the year 800, Bagdad was the heart of the Moslem empire, a gorgeous new city with "tall towers that amazed the moon" built on an ancient site. There in a luxurious palace, rich with azure and gold, dwelt the Caliph Harun al Rashid (Aaron the Just), surrounded by artists and scholars—he himself a poet, scholar, statesman and fabulous hero of the Arabian Nights, which were written at this time.

Harun al Rashid

The year 800 had barely passed when to the ear of the Caliph in Bagdad came strange news from Rome. A king of the Franks, grandson and namesake of Charles the Hammer, had been crowned Roman Emperor by the Pope! What was the meaning? Was the Roman Empire to be revived? With a barbarian king for emperor? How would that strike the Emperor at Constantinople, head of the eastern part of the Roman Empire which had never been destroyed? The Caliph drew thoughtfully on his water pipe and meditated. He had completed satisfactory dealings with the East. To Charlemagne, the new Emperor of the West, he would dispatch gifts—an elephant, a water clock, and above all, keys to the holy places in Jerusalem, with assurance that his Christian subjects were free to come on pilgrimage.

This is his signature.
(The "A" is in the center.)

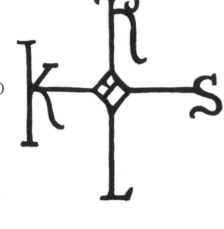

Charlemagne, great King of the Franks, was no such scholar as the fabulous Caliph with whom he exchanged gifts and greetings. Yet he could speak and read Latin, kept trying to learn to write, and was well educated for those dark days in Europe when even writing monks often copied the shapes of words without knowing how to read them. And for any day and age he was an outstanding statesman, with a genuine love for law and order.

The most glorious moment of his life came on Christmas Day of the year 800. As he knelt at mass in old St. Peter's in Rome, he felt a crown being placed upon his head and heard the people shout, "Long life to Carolus Augustus, Emperor of the Romans, crowned by God!" A Roman Emperor!

Then his was a Roman Empire! For thirty years he had worked and thought and fought to create such an empire out of the vast territory of the tribes which he had inherited. By almost constant war, he had conquered and added all the barbarian tribes along the border of his land, to prevent it from being invaded by them and destroyed. It was a vast, unwieldy realm—a conglomeration of people, speaking various languages, using primitive German customs in the north, clinging to remnants of old Roman laws in the south. To attempt to unite them had been a tre-

Charlemagne :

King of the Franks rules as a Roman Emperor.

mendous undertaking, but Charlemagne worked out an efficient system. First he issued uniform laws on every kind of subject, in one decree, even mentioning what to do with surplus hens' eggs. To enforce the laws, he appointed special officers called counts to rule various districts. To keep watch over them, he sent out traveling inspectors in pairs—a count and a bishop, who became known as the "Emperor's Eyes."

Once a year the Lord Emperor himself took counsel with the people in a great National Assembly, held outdoors in a field, each May. It was like the ancient tribal assembly of his German ancestors. However, it was too huge, included too many people for each one to attend individually. So a new system came into being whereby one or two men were sent to speak for a whole tribe, or represent a county or district. This was the beginning of the representative system, which we use today, and without which the great free republics of our modern world would be impossible.

Charlemagne's capital city was Aix, or Aachen, near the river Rhine. It was there in his palace that he started a famous school for the children and sent abroad for the best teachers he could find. One was a monk from England, where learning had spread from the old monasteries in Ireland which had never been destroyed.

Also from England was a wide-eyed young prince, Egbert of Wessex. He had been driven out by some of the Saxon kings who were forever at war. When Egbert was able to return home, he went, filled with ambition to conquer and unite those warring Saxons, and become a great king like Charlemagne.

Feudalism

Charlemagne died in 814 and when the firm hand of the absolute ruler relaxed its hold, order resolved into chaos. His vast Empire, divided among his three jealous grandsons, fell apart into a thousand pieces. Counts who had been given land, hung onto it. Others grabbed as much land as they could by fair means or foul. Each one then hied himself to a steep hill, built himself a castle on top, walled it in, surrounded the wall with a ditch of water, drew up the bridge, and prepared to defend himself and his land against all comers. Smaller landowners, clinging to what they had, hopeless of saving their land or their lives, ran to a strong man for protection, acknowledged him as their lord, put their hands in his, became his vassals—his fighting men. That was feudalism, a social order based on "feud," the old German word for "owning land." Feudalism was better than anarchy (no order at all) and probably more agreeable to the semi-civilized Franks than the law and order imposed upon them by Charlemagne. After all they were independent fellows, those Franks, not used to

Feudalism brings some law and order out of chaos.

taking orders. Fighting was their old way of life—under a chief of their own choosing.

While the feudal lord and his vassals fought, the actual work of the land was done by serfs who were bound to it and sold with it, like the trees and the grass, but not sold separately, like slaves.

The law of the land? Various and haphazard. The decrees of the old counts and landlords, the regulations of bishops and abbots, and for judgment of crimes, the crude old German customs of ordeal and trial by combat, which were also to be used in England for another 500 years.

Ordeal:
A person accused of a crime was obliged to prove himself innocent. After appealing to Heaven, he carried a piece of red-hot iron a certain distance, or plunged his arm into boiling water. If, after several days, there was no severe burn, he was judged innocent.

Another test was to throw a man into a pond. If he sank, and had to be rescued, he was innocent. If he floated, that is if the pure water wouldn't take him, he was guilty.

Trial by Combat:
A man who was accused, could challenge the one who accused him to fight to the death. The victor was innocent because God had singled out the righteous man and given the victory to him.

ALFRED

battles the Danes.

England had been in great danger when Egbert returned home from the court of Charlemagne to become the King of Wessex. Danes—pagan pirates from the North Sea—were raiding the east coast, sweeping in over the countryside, destroying churches and monasteries, slaying priests, sparing no one. Fear for their very lives forced the Saxon kings to stop fighting one another and unite under Egbert against the fury of the Northmen. But like waves of the sea, the Northmen came again, and doubtless would have conquered all of England had it not been for Alfred, grandson of Egbert, who came to be known as Alfred the Great.

DANELAW

WALES

ESSEX

KENT

SUSSEX

◨ ALFRED'S KINGDOM

Many tales are told of Alfred's desperate struggle against the Danes. How he fled with a small band through swamps and moors and tangled woods. How he was hidden in the hut of a herdsman, and burned the good wife's cakes. How he went as a spy into the camp of the Danes, disguised as a minstrel. How he finally defeated the Danish King enough to make him agree to a treaty whereby he and his Danes were to have a section of land on the east of the island and were to live there under their own laws, the Dane laws.

A white horse was Alfred's symbol. Cut into a green hillside in Wiltshire may still be seen the shape of a horse in white stone, 180 feet long, thought to commemorate Alfred's victory over the Danes.

Alfred rules his people wisely and well.

After the settlement, Alfred turned his attention to repairing the damage done by the Danes, to improving education and administering justice, and to putting his kingdom in order.

He himself studied and mastered Latin grammar in order to translate the history of the Anglo-Saxon (the Anglo-Saxon Chronicle) written by the Venerable Bede into the language of the people.

Alfred also collected and had written down the Anglo-Saxon laws, headed by the Ten Commandments and ending with the Golden Rule and these words: "He who keep these shall need no other Law Book."

Alfred was a good king, a brave man who gave as his only wish "to live worthily and leave my memory in good works." He died in 899, more than 1000 years ago. His descendants still occupy the throne.

the Great Anglo-Saxon

In the year 1000 bold Vikings touched the shores of North America

In the year 1003, a Viking, Sweyn the Dane, conquered England and "all the people," says the Anglo-Saxon Chronicle, "held him for full king."

Over 100 years before that, Norsemen in their dragon-headed ships had ravaged the coasts of France. Soon after Charlemagne died, they were riding into Aachen, stabling their stolen horses in his church. And Rolf the Ganger, son of a mighty jarl of Norway, was sailing into the Seine and up the river toward Paris, main city of the feudal lord who held the rather worthless title of "King" among the Franks.

In 911 it was Charles the Simple, great great grandson of Charlemagne, who held the doubtful honor. Shivering in his boots, he made a bargain with mighty Rolf the Ganger to give him a Dukedom of land, and a wife, provided he would settle down, become a Christian, and acknowledge himself the King's vassal. To this the sturdy Viking agreed. But as for kissing the foot of his royal over-lord in the feudal ceremony, he would have none of it! One of his warriors assigned to do so for him, jerked up the royal foot and tipped the simpleton over backwards amid loud roars of laughter.

The land given to Rolf and his Northmen became Normandy. There, about 1028, William, the great great great grandson of old Rolf, was born, to be the young duke of Normandy and become William the Conqueror of England.

sailing westward under Leif the Lucky and called it Vinland the Good.

William's story begins with his great aunt Emma who was married to the Anglo-Saxon King, when Sweyn the Dane conquered England, took the throne and sent Emma flying back home to Normandy with her young son, Prince Edward.

Edward, a mild, meek lad, grew into a mild, meek, pious young man. He was very different from his violent, precocious young cousin William who was fifteen when Edward received word to return to England to be King. Edward spoke French—not Anglo-Saxon—and would have made a far better monk, but the Witenagemot had chosen him for King, and King he was for twenty-four years. On his death bed, having no son, he recommended his wife's brother, Harold, for King to the Witenagemot. They approved, and Harold, Earl of Essex, was crowned.

When this word reached Normandy, William the Duke was so furious "that no man dare speak to him." All the wild blood of his Viking ancestors pounded in his ears. Edward had promised the throne of England to him. Harold himself had sworn over sacred saint's bones that it should be his. What was to be his should still be his!

Shipbuilders were set to work; smiths put to making lances, swords, helmets, and coats of mail; archers and cavalry equipped. And in the fall of 1066, William, Duke of Normandy, sailed forth on what was to be the last invasion of England. Actually this was nothing but a large scale raid on the part of those Norman barons who followed William to get a fair share of the land, which he promised to give them after he had won the kingdom from Harold.

William, the Norman

These are scenes from the famous old Bayeux Tapestry, embroidered about 1170, showing the conquest of England. Harold is warned of approaching evil. William rides aboard his dragon-headed ships. The battle rages between Norman cavalry and Anglo-Saxon foot soldiers with their battleaxes.

WILLIAM:

Harold, the last Anglo-Saxon King, died on the battlefield of Hastings. When his foot soldiers with their clumsy battleaxes fell before the Norman bowmen and cavalry, Anglo-Saxon England ended and Norman England began. When William the Conqueror rode from the battlefield to the city of London, the Witenagemot could but open the gates and offer him the crown. There, on Christmas day of 1066, in Westminster Abbey (newly built by his cousin Edward), William the Norman became King of the English. And "so stern and wrathful was he that none durst do anything against his will." So says the Anglo-Saxon Chronicle. The Saxon nobles who resisted him he treated as rebels, took their lands and gave them to his Norman barons.

The English landowners who were left became Norman vassals. Poorer farmers became either serfs, bound to the land, or slaves locked in iron collars. And looking down upon them all were these haughty French-speaking foreign barons, high and mighty as their castles of stone that rose across the land, or the new stone Tower of London dominating the city.

William ruled these Norman barons also with a strong hand. He did not propose to have such disorder as existed in France, where feudal lords with their armies of vassals were as powerful as the one who was called "King." He intended to give England the law and order needed for peace and prosperity. Therefore, like a clear-headed executive, he had a survey

made of the whole realm so that he should know exactly what land each man owned and what was on it. The results were recorded in what people called a Doomsday Book, because, as on the final day of doom, nobody or nothing escaped being numbered. "Not a rood of land, not a peasant's hut, not an ox pig, or even a hive of bees escaped." That done, William called a meeting of all the landowners and their vassals and made every one of them bow before him and swear direct allegiance to him as Lord, King and supreme ruler.

William was stern and willful, but he was just and fair and gave England unity and order without destroying the old common laws, village moots or Witenagemot.

Quite naturally the Normans long thought of Normandy as "home," but in time that feeling passed. They began to speak Anglo-Saxon, and the Anglo-Saxons began to use French words.

And so gradually was completed that blend of Britons, Jutes, Saxons, Angles, Danes and Normans who were to be known as English.

William the Conqueror died in 1087, just eight years before the first of those expeditions to the Holy Land known as Crusades.

More powerful than any king in the days of William the Conqueror was the Pope, Gregory VII, who also lived just before the first Crusade. Even the German King, then known as the Holy Roman Emperor, stood barefooted in the snow three days waiting to beg forgiveness of the Pope after being excommunicated by him for disobeying his commands.

Gregory VII saw the power of the Pope as far above the power of a king as the soul of man was superior to his body, or life in heaven to this life on earth, which to every medieval man was but a prelude to that awful judgment day whose horrors were plainly pictured on the stone walls of his church. There souls heavy with sin were being dragged off by fiends to fiery and eternal torture, while winged angels were leading the blessed ones to heaven. Every man from king to peasant was haunted by the fear of that final day. Only by obeying the rules of the church, by praying and fasting when the bells rang, by making pilgrimages to the shrine of a saint, could one hope to reduce the burden of his sin. Most blessed were they who could make the pilgrimage to Holy Jerusalem.

Crusades +

Although for 500 years Jerusalem had been under the empire of Islam, Christians had been making that holy pilgrimage unmolested by the cultured Arabs. But shortly before Gregory VII died, barbarous Turks from Asia, Moslems too fiercely devout to respect the faith of Christian "infidels," barred the way to Jerusalem. In 1095 the Emperor of the East sent out a cry for help to the new Pope Urban II, who passed on the cry to his own people, the Franks:

"O race of Franks! Beloved and chosen of God! From the confines of Jerusalem and from Constantinople a grievous report has gone forth that an accursed race wholly alienated from God has invaded these lands. Let your own quarrels end. Wrest that land from the wicked race and subject it to yourselves. Undertake this journey eagerly for the remission of your sins and imperishable glory in the kingdom of Heaven."

What an appeal! Who could resist it? From all over Europe, all classes of people responded. Three kings joined in the third Crusade: the King of France, the Roman Emperor of Germany, and the King of England, that glamorous, quarrelsome young ruffian, Richard the Lion-Hearted, who to his amazement found Saladin the Sultan most cultured and chivalrous, even though an "infidel." What they learned and saw in the East opened the eyes and minds of all those rough untutored Europeans. Those feudal knights who lived only to fight, returned from the East with new respect for learning, and new ideas from a way of living other than their own. The Crusades marked a turning point for Europe from the Dark Ages toward the light. They helped set Europe free, but not Jerusalem.

Magna Carta

English noblemen demand their rights.

Richard the Lion-Hearted left his brother John behind in England when he went off to the Crusades. John laughed a mean treacherous laugh when he heard that Richard was imprisoned in Germany on his way home, and hoped he would never escape. Later, when he was King, John made probably the worst King that England ever had. He quarreled with the French King and lost Normandy. He quarreled with the

at Runnymede

signed in the Year 1215

Pope, was excommunicated and practically had to buy back his crown. He vented his spleen on the bishops and cut off their revenue. He taxed the barons unmercifully, wasted their money and demanded more. He had innocent persons who displeased him seized and thrown into prison without trial. In every way he was brutal, cruel, treacherous—in short, a tyrant.

The nobles and bishops finally and rightfully rebelled against this tyranny. They claimed certain rights they had had in the past. They determined to force the King to sign a written guarantee of those rights or declare war against him. Two thousand knights in armor attended the barons and bishops when they met the King with their demands. He was furious, but helpless. What could he do but agree to meet them at the appointed time and place? Therefore, on June 15 in the year 1215, in a tent pitched on the south side of the river Thames, in a meadow called Runnymede, a bad King shaking with fury signed the first great document of English liberties.

Taxes:

No taxes were to be levied on nobles, except by consent of the Great Council (the old Witenagemot), which was composed of nobles and bishops.

Trial:

No one was to be arrested, imprisoned or punished except after trial by his equals according to the law of the land. (The old ordeals and trial by battle were now being abolished for trial by jury which would be established by 1350.) Justice was not to be sold, denied or delayed.

by John, the King

The Great Charter was signed, giving nobles and bishops the rights they asked for. But how many nobles and bishops were there in England or any other land compared to the number of serfs? Very few. When the Crusades began, about five-sixths of the people in England were serfs. Fortunately for them, the Crusades were costly expeditions to equip. To raise the huge sums of money needed, Richard the Lion-Hearted and other great feudal lords sold towns their freedom. That helped free many serfs. For artisans and craftsmen living in the town which had grown up around the lord's castle were serfs, just as much as the farmers who tilled the soil.

But once a town had purchased its freedom, once it had a precious charter written and signed giving it the right of self-government, its citizens were free. Any serf who escaped to a free town and lived there for a year and a day could never be reclaimed by his former lord and master. He was a freeman—free to choose a trade, join a trade guild and support himself. And for a time a towns-man had no worry about taxes. Only the land was taxed. Barons and bishops owned the land, so they paid the taxes.

However, in time personal property also came to be taxed. Then the prosper-

WNS :

Townsmen buy their freedom and gain a place in Parliament.

Parliament

ous craftsmen and merchants were as anxious to have a say about taxes as the barons and bishops. But to do that they, as well as the barons and bishops, had to be represented in the Witenagemot, which was now being called by the French name—Parliament. That, too, came about.

Henry III, the worthless son of King John, first swore to uphold the Great Charter, then broke his oath, loaded the barons with unjust taxes until they rebelled, and this time rebellion led to war. Simon de Montfort, the King's brother-in-law, was the leader. There was a battle in which 15,000 townsmen from London joined the barons. The King was taken prisoner. That left Simon able to summon Parliament, which he did. But the King's friends were hostile, and de Montfort needed all the support that he could get. So he called not only the barons and bishops to his Parliament, but also two knights from each county and two citizens from each town! And this, in 1265, was the beginning of the House of Commons. Simon de Montfort was killed by jealous barons, but what he started lived on. Edward I, the next King, unlike his father and grandfather, was a good King and a statesman. In 1295 he called a Parliament in which all classes of freemen were represented and which was then divided into the House of Commons and the House of Lords, as it still remains to this day.

freedom

I n the autumn of 1245 a young Italian friar with an older companion was trudging on toward Paris, making the long journey from Italy to Paris on foot. The young, very fat friar was Thomas Aquinas, related to half the kings of Europe, and a very brilliant scholar. He was headed for the great gathering place for students, famous since 1200 as the University of Paris. He found the lecture halls on the left of the river, across from the island and the cathedral of Notre Dame, just completed with new high pointed Gothic arches. New also and most exciting was the subject for study—the works of the ancient Greek philosopher, ARISTOTLE! Not in the original, but in a translation into Latin made from a translation into Arabic, acquired from the Moslems. The fascinating, all-absorbing argument was how Aristotle's answers to such questions as to how and when the world was created could be made to fit with the teaching of the church. Could they be? Yes, answered Thomas Aquinas, and with his precise, logical mind proceeded to do so, as thoroughly, ingeniously and brilliantly as possible.

to think?

Roger Bacon, a young English friar with a fine, inquiring mind, studied in Paris ten years before Thomas Aquinas. He was bored by the incessant repetition of what Aristotle had said, or was supposed to have said. Who could tell? Could any one read Greek? Could any one read Arabic, to test the translation? No. Moreover, how did those ancient Greek philosophers come by the ideas which Aristotle had recorded? By using their minds, by observing, experimenting! And so did Roger Bacon. He returned to England's new university at Oxford, and in 1250 published his findings in chemistry and light. He was accused of using "black magic, the devil's art," and spent the next ten years practically in prison, or deprived of books and instruments. A simple man was not free to question or explore. All knowledge had been summed up in the teaching of the Church and the science of Aristotle and walled in like a medieval fortress. Within those limits a scholar might wander about among the ideas, arrange and rearrange them. But go outside? No. That was forbidden and dangerous ground—the territory of the devil.

Death of

Gunpowder makes feudal warfare useless.
Black Death helps free the serfs.
French King overpowers the lords.

The Hundred Years War between France and England began in 1338. With the famous battle at Crécy, in 1346, the downfall of feudalism began. There for the first time, common peasants fighting on foot were able to stand their ground against feudal lords on horseback. The victorious peasants were English farmers armed with a tremendous bow from which a blizzard of arrows blinding the French knights pierced their metal armor and brought them to the ground.

On that famous battlefield there also appeared a new weapon. "A small bombard" it was called "which with fire and noise like unto God's thunder threw little balls to frighten the horses." That was all, then. But behind those little balls was GUNPOWDER! And later, its use would make common men able to shatter those castle walls that had protected the feudal lords and bring their way of living to an end.

Meanwhile, during the Hundred Years War, peasants, taxed unmercifully by their overlords to pay for the cost, rose in frantic rebellion both in France and England, but to no avail. Help came, however, in a strange way. A hideous plague, known as the Black Death, swept over Europe. Thousands died. Labor became so scarce that serfs and slaves escaping were able to get work and to be paid as freemen.

Feudalism

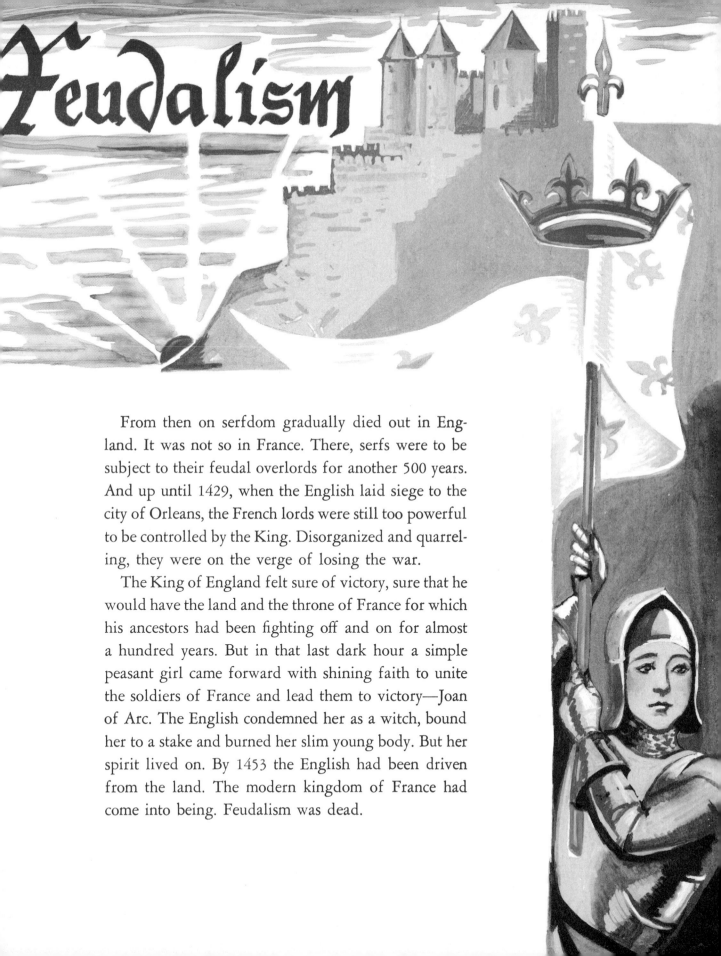

From then on serfdom gradually died out in England. It was not so in France. There, serfs were to be subject to their feudal overlords for another 500 years. And up until 1429, when the English laid siege to the city of Orleans, the French lords were still too powerful to be controlled by the King. Disorganized and quarreling, they were on the verge of losing the war.

The King of England felt sure of victory, sure that he would have the land and the throne of France for which his ancestors had been fighting off and on for almost a hundred years. But in that last dark hour a simple peasant girl came forward with shining faith to unite the soldiers of France and lead them to victory—Joan of Arc. The English condemned her as a witch, bound her to a stake and burned her slim young body. But her spirit lived on. By 1453 the English had been driven from the land. The modern kingdom of France had come into being. Feudalism was dead.

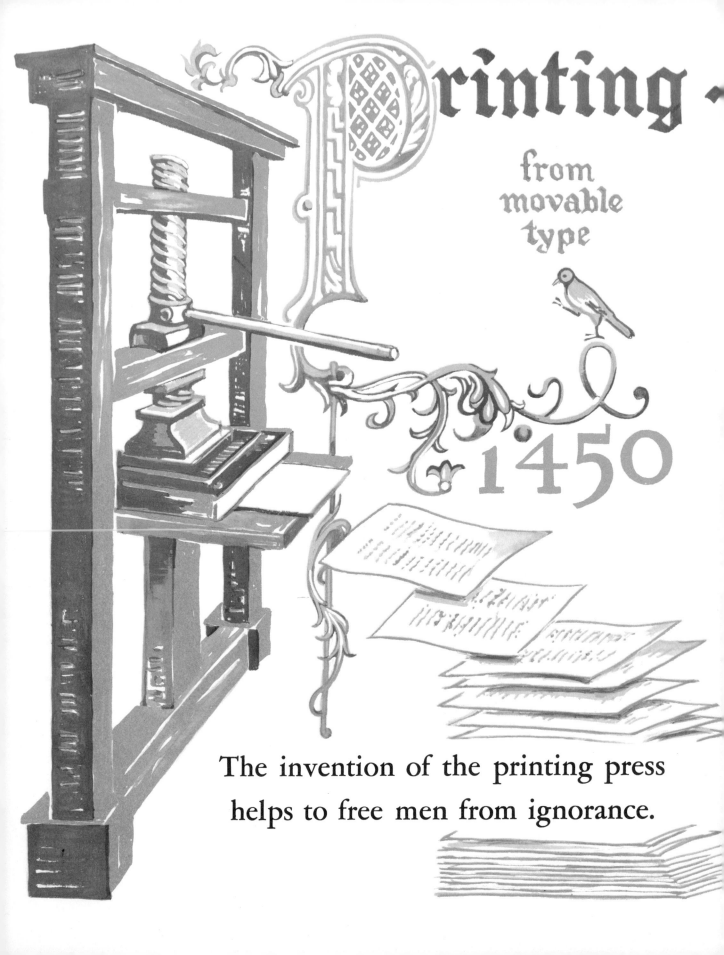

Printing

from movable type

1450

The invention of the printing press
helps to free men from ignorance.

by Johannes Gutenberg,

Between 1450 and 1453, in the German town of Mainz, Johannes Gutenberg stood beside his new printing press, laid a sheet of dampened paper over a block of type, and soon held in his hand the first page of his first printed book. This was what he had dreamed of and worked toward for years, a way of making books that would be accurate and fast and cheap. Now it was here. For when enough copies of this page had been printed, the type could be broken apart, the letters quickly rearranged into other words to print the next page and the next. This page, unlike all others before it, had not been printed from one solid block of wood. Every single letter was on its own separate block. That was Gutenberg's invention. That was the idea he had worked to perfect through long discouraging years, believing that in this way books could be made fast enough and cheap enough for everyone to have them. Books hand copied by the monks were so slow to make and so costly that even the wealthy seldom owned more than one or two. True, they were beautiful. Yet beautiful, too, was this newly printed page. One could scarcely see the difference, so exactly had Gutenberg followed the heavy Gothic letters used by the German monks.

News of his invention spread. The King of France (whom Joan of Arc had seen crowned) sent the maker of his money to learn the new art. Three of Gutenberg's pupils went to set up a press at the University of Paris. They had to be protected however from many who feared such magical work must be the work of the devil. Printers from Mainz also went to Italy, where they designed the type which we still use—the slanting Italic and the straight Roman.

An envoy of the Pope, traveling in Germany in 1454, was quick to take advantage of Gutenberg's invention. The Pope was calling for help against the Turks, offering the same inducements as in the days of the Crusades. Gutenberg was asked to print the notices. Danger from the Turks was very serious. The year before, using gunpowder and cannon balls, they had succeeded in breaking through the old walls of Constantinople, and brought to an end the Roman Empire of the East, in 1453.

So, with the end of feudalism, the use of gunpowder, the invention of the printing press, the Middle Ages end. And, almost 1000 years from the Fall of Rome, the modern world begins with a great rebirth of learning and freedom, known as the Renaissance.

The RENAI

It was in Italy that the Renaissance began. There, where fragments of Greek and Roman civilization still remained, it came to life again. Ancient master-pieces of sculpture buried in overgrown ruins were un-earthed. Old books lost for 1000 years were rediscov-ered in monasteries. From Constantinople, Greek schol-ars fleeing from the Turks sought refuge in Italy and brought with them priceless manuscripts which were translated into Latin, and later into the language spoken by the people. The first great writer to write only in this Italian language was the poet Dante, who was born as the Crusades were ending and the Middle Ages drawing to a close.

Men of the new free age of learning looked to the past and also to the future, eager to know and do and enjoy everything in what again seemed to them, as to the ancient Greeks, a beautiful world.

The one man who most nearly expressed the whole inquiring spirit of the new age was Leonardo da Vinci, painter, sculptor, architect, engineer and, above all, philosopher. He was born in 1452 near the city of

IN ITALY

Florence, known as the "cradle of the Renaissance." That is where it began. There the arts were nurtured and the artists encouraged and supported by a powerful and wealthy family of bankers, the Medici.

Cosimo I, who established the rule of his family in Florence, welcomed the Greek refugees and kept them busy making books for his new library. His grandson, Lorenzo "the Magnificent," himself a poet and a scholar, had the gardens of his palace filled with Greek and Roman sculpture. There young Michelangelo went to study when he was fourteen, just the age of Lorenzo's own son, who later became Pope Leo X, and who then, after 1500, made Rome the new center of the Renaissance. At the same time, the "new learning" spread from Italy to all other countries of Europe and into every field of knowledge.

In 1543, Copernicus, a Pole, announced the startling discovery that the sun, not the earth, was the center of the universe, which Galileo proved a century later.

Prince Henry "the Navigator," of Portugal, prepared the way for exploration. A new way to India had to be found for European merchants by sea now that the old overland routes were blocked by the fearful Turks.

In 1492 another Italian, sailing westward from Spain in search of that way to India, discovered a new world.

ROME

Europeans discover a new and unexplored world.

The year 1492 was a triumphant year for Spain and its two Catholic sovereigns Ferdinand and Isabella. On the second day of the year the Moslems, after being gradually pushed out of Spain, were forced to surrender their last stronghold of Granada. So fiercely exalted was Isabella at being free of the Moslem menace, that she determined for the good of Spain to weed out all other religions foreign to her own, that of the Jews especially. To do this she revived a cruel persecution known as the Inquisition.

Also, in 1492, as soon as possible after the Moslem surrender, Isabella gave her support to the daringly attractive project of an Italian navigator who proposed to sail west from Spain around the world to India. She furnished him with three ships, and in October, 1492, Christopher Columbus sailed. Queen Isabella's support of Columbus, though it failed in the original purpose, gave

TURKS BLOCK THE WAY EAST

HOLLAND

FRANCE

SPAIN

GENOA

ITALY

Constantinople

from Palos

Spain the first foothold in the new world, filled her treasury to overflowing with gold, and made her for a time the richest nation in Europe.

A great new continent! When it was found that this was what Columbus had discovered, the scramble was on between the nations of Europe to get their share of this fabulous new land. The King of England, Henry VII, who had refused to speculate on Columbus, now financed John Cabot, another Italian navigator, who by 1498 had made two voyages along the coast of North America and claimed it for England.

"Show me the clause in the will of Father Adam," cried Francis I, the King of France, "which divides America between you two and excludes the French." He, too, hired an Italian, followed by French explorers, who staked claims in North America, from the mouth of the St. Lawrence River toward the center of the continent, calling it New France.

Portugal, also, long interested and active in this great age of exploration, divided with Spain the continent of South America.

America? That name for the new world was first used by a German map maker, because Americus Vespucius, another Italian, after exploring the coast of South America, was the first to declare that what his friend Columbus had discovered actually *was* a new world.

Charles V · · Pope Leo X ·

The absolute rule of the Roman Church is broken as

The absolute rule of the Church, which had reached a peak during the Crusades, grew weaker, and finally ended in 1520 when one man dared defy the two greatest powers in his world, the Pope and the Emperor. The Emperor was young Charles V, grandson of Ferdinand and Isabella, who at sixteen became heir to all the vast possessions of Spain. Four years later, in 1520, as heir to his other grandfather, Maximilian of Austria, Charles was elected by the German princes to be the Holy Roman Emperor. The next year young Charles held his first Diet, or meeting, of the German princes and bishops in the city of Worms. There to appear before them came a monk, Martin Luther, who had been threatened with excommunication by Pope Leo X.

Leo X, the son of Lorenzo de' Medici, was an indolent, softly fat man, devoted to art, music, literature and good food, and always in need of money to indulge his tastes, and also to continue the magnificent rebuilding of St. Peter's Cathedral. Now during the Crusades those who could not do penance for their sins by going, could do so by helping pay the expenses. Leo X followed the same pattern, offering similar "Indulgences" for sale, which his agents falsely represented as sure passports to heaven.

Martin Luther · · Henry VIII

a German monk protests and an English king rebels.

Martin Luther, who taught at the German University of Wittenberg, was shocked that instead of being taught the value of faith and inward goodness, people were being told to buy their way out of sin. He spoke against this in a series of debates that roused all Europe. He burned the papal decree threatening excommunication and at the Diet of Worms refused to recant, saying "to go against one's conscience is neither right nor safe." Later, hidden in the Prince's castle in Saxony, Luther translated the New Testament into German, and laid the foundation of the Church that was to bear his name and spread through northern Europe.

Pope Adrian VI, the next Pope, was a sincerely devout man. "God has allowed this chastisement to come upon His Church," he said, "because of the sins of priests and prelates. We know that for many years much to be regarded with horror has come to pass."

Henry VIII was not quite eighteen when in 1509 he became King of England. His wife, six years older than he, was Catharine of Aragon, aunt of Charles V who visited them in London in 1520, the year that Luther burned the papal decree. Henry VIII published a reply to Luther which so delighted Leo X that he gave him the title of "Defender of the Faith," praising him for his "angelic spirit." Twenty years later Henry VIII was excommunicated for divorcing Catharine. Therefore, glad to close the monasteries and get the wealth and tax-free lands of the church under his control, Henry forced the English bishops and Parliament to declare him, and not the Pope, head of the National church of England. As defender of the Faith, he prohibited all Protestant teaching. And he married four more wives before he died. His daughter by Anne Boleyn was born in 1533 and christened Elizabeth.

England's Queen Elizabeth I watches as

Queen Elizabeth, daughter of Henry VIII, vain, high-spirited, fiery-tempered as her red hair, liked men, loved England, was adored by her subjects but told Parliament firmly that she intended to remain a virgin. Of all impossible suitors, none was more distasteful to her than Philip II, the King of Spain. Chilly, overbearing, self-righteous creature, with his huge chin and bulging eyes! Elizabeth knew very well that by marrying her, Philip hoped to turn England back into a Catholic country, under the Pope.

Philip II did indeed consider himself the invincible champion of the Church. He was prepared to stamp out opposition anywhere by any method necessary in the vast possessions which he had inherited from his father, Charles V. And so he lost the provinces that his father loved most—the low flat land along the North Sea, known as the Netherlands, or Holland. Into this land from Germany the teachings of Luther and other Protestants had "flowed like the waters of the Rhine," and been accepted by many. Among them were the parents of William, Prince of Orange, who as a boy had been brought up as a page in the household of Charles V. A sincere, energetic man, William "the Silent" truly believed in religious freedom. To his horror he saw the Spanish Inquisition brought into Holland—people burned at the stake, beheaded, buried alive!

little Holland wins freedom from Spain.

He saw churches destroyed and monasteries wrecked in retaliation. Then he saw Philip put a Duke in control whose rule was so unendurable that Catholics and Protestants united. In 1581, under the leadership of William of Orange, the brave people of the Netherlands rose against the tyranny of Spain with this declaration of independence:

> "Whereas God did not create the people slaves to their prince to obey his commands whether right or wrong, but rather the prince for the sake of the subjects, to govern them with equity, to love and support them as a father his children or a shepherd his flock, (therefore) when he does not behave thus, but oppresses them, seeking to infringe on their ancient customs and privileges, then he is no longer a prince but a tyrant, and the subjects may legally proceed to the choice of another prince for their defence."

Queen Elizabeth came to the aid of the New Republic of the Netherlands first secretly, then openly. In 1584 she learned that William of Orange had been killed. In that year the Virgin Queen received with pleasure Walter Raleigh's report of the colony which he had founded in America. It was named for her— Virginia.

James I

Parliament looked for the nearest heir to the throne after Elizabeth died. It called James Stuart, son of Mary Queen of Scots, and made him James I of England.

A shrewd, conceited man he was, with a small narrow mind so overly crammed with facts that he did not hesitate to bring forth the final word on every possible subject. His favorite topic was the Divine Right of Kings. In fact, as a king, James considered himself second only to God. "Kings," he said, "are God's lieutenants on earth and sit upon God's throne. God makes the king and the king makes the law." This was an odd sounding speech to members of Parliament who had chosen him to be King. They protested and insisted on their rights. James dismissed Parliament and let it stay dismissed for seven years, while he thought up tricky ways to get money. His last years were spent in over-eating and over-drinking until death removed him from the throne, leaving it to his son Charles I who married Henrietta Maria, royal princess of France.

son of

Charles I   Henrietta

Their children

Charles II

Mary

James II

married
WILLIAM II
of
HOLLAND

Their son

WILLIAM III married   Mary

daughter of

They ruled England
as

William and Mary

Henry IV

daughter of

Maria

son of

Louis XIII

son of

Louis XIV

Henry IV was one of the best and best loved kings of France. Henrietta Maria did not remember her father, as she was but a year old when he was assassinated by a religious fanatic. His death was doubly tragic, since Henry IV was the first King in modern Europe to issue a declaration of religious freedom—the famous Edict of Nantes. All his young life Henry had seen France torn apart by civil war in which religion and politics were mixed. He had lived through the hideous St. Bartholomew's massacre of Huguenots (French Protestants). He had been opposed by two other Henrys fighting for the throne before he became King. What France needed was to be united. To do this Henry IV, a Protestant, accepted the Catholic faith which predominated, and then issued the declaration of freedom to protect the Huguenots.

His grandson Louis XIV, unfortunately revoked the Edict. He also established the Divine Right of Kings in France, while his cousins in England were being forced to recognize the divine rights of the People.

THE PORTRAICTUER OF CAPTAYNE JOHN SMITH, ADMIRALL OF NEW ENGLAND

LONDON COMPANY

Chesapeake Bay

the Potomac

o JAMESTOWN

the James

English settlers carry their rights and

Jamestown, the first permanent colony in Virginia, was named for James I, and was a business venture. A company of London "gentlemen" obtained a charter from King James, giving them the right to settle in Virginia, in return for one fifth of all gold or precious metals they should find. In May, 1607, these gentlemen were sailing into a Virginia river, to be named the James, and there planted a feeble colony.

According to the Charter, the colony was to be governed by a council appointed by the King and all settlers were to enjoy the rights of Englishmen in England. As it did not say how these "gentlemen" settlers who had never worked with their hands were to stay alive in the wilderness, it was fortunate that there was among them an enter-

prising young leader, Captain John Smith. And there was tobacco! Although described by King James as a "loathsome vile weed," it brought him far from loathsome revenue.

Also, according to the charter, the church of England was to be established in Virginia. That was especially important to the King, because of what was happening in England. There, certain independent church members called Puritans, proposed to "purify" the church ceremony, do away with images, incense, mitres, robes and even bishops. James I was infuriated. He vowed to make those Puritan "vipers" conform or "harry them out of the land." He fined, imprisoned and persecuted them until a small group from Scrooby village, known as the Separatists, left England and

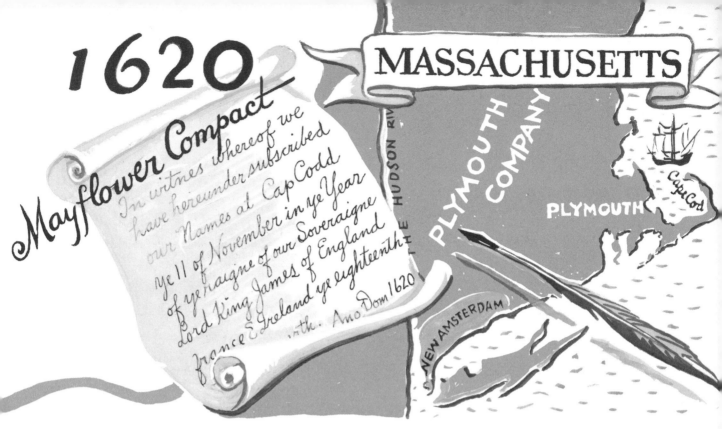

1620

MASSACHUSETTS

Mayflower Compact

In witnes whereof we have hereunder subscribed our Names at Cap Codd ye 11 of November in ye Year of ye raigne of our Soveraigne Lord King James of England France & Ireland ye eighteenth . . . .th. Ano Dom 1620

THE HUDSON RIVER

PLYMOUTH COMPANY

PLYMOUTH

Cap Cod

NEW AMSTERDAM

customs to the New World.

went as pilgrims to Holland where "men were free to worship as they chose." There in Holland they were contented for eleven years until, as William Bradford said, their "reverend pastor and grave elder Brewster" feared that they might forget their own language did they not leave Holland and go on as pilgrims to another land.

By that time Henry Hudson, employed by Holland, had discovered a river in America and the Dutch had founded the colony of New Netherlands. Just to the north lay the land to which the Pilgrims planned to go. A London company going for fish and furs agreed to take them on their ship, the *Mayflower,* sailing from Plymouth, England, September 21, 1620. Three months later, the little band of Pil-

grims and the others, landed on the bleak wintry shore of New England. One of the elders carried a rolled paper on which were rules for governing the colony written by the Pilgrim fathers and signed in the cabin of the ship—the Mayflower Compact. All matters for the general good, it said, were to be discussed in Town Meeting—the old Anglo-Saxon "moot" in the new world.

This was the most democratic, but not the first, government established in the English colonies of America. The first was the House of Burgesses in Virginia, formed in 1619. This, like the House of Commons at home, was made up of representatives of the people to work with the royal governor who represented and was appointed by the King.

PURITANS

Charles I

Charles I was completely dishonest in dealing with the House of Commons. He promised one thing and did the opposite, believing the people had no right to question or make demands of a king. There were many Puritans in the House of Commons. They were suspicious when Charles I married Henrietta Maria, a French Catholic, that he would favor the Catholics, which he promised not to do, but did. He further antagonized the Puritans by forbidding their own preachers to explain the teaching of the Church. He also encouraged dancing on the green and playing games after Sunday service, insulting the Puritans, who would not even cook a meal on the Sabbath day.

"There is no place for us but the wilderness," concluded John Winthrop, a wealthy Puritan of Suffolk. Seven hundred others, many graduates of Oxford and Cambridge, quite the "best people," left with him for the new world. There in 1630, on Massachusetts Bay, they founded a Puritan Commonwealth, for Puritans only, where only church members could vote. That was Boston.

Roger Williams, a young minister who believed in true freedom of soul, was driven out into the winter woods and later founded the town of Providence, Rhode Island. The first declaration of freedom for all Christian settlers in America was made in 1634 by Lord Calvert, a Catholic, who ruled like a feudal lord over land granted him by Charles I and named for the Queen, Henrietta Maria—land of Maria, or Maryland.

Friction, meanwhile, between Parliament and the King increased until one fatal day of 1642 when Charles I walked into the House of Commons to seize five members by armed force. That was the final outrage against the liberties of the people. That led to war!

behead the King- and then what?

Oliver Cromwell, a Puritan, a Commoner, a man of great integrity, organized and commanded the Puritan army, which defeated that of the King. Charles I, condemned as a tyrant and public enemy, was sentenced to death. On January 30, 1649, the King's head fell from the bloody block in front of the royal palace in London, "as a lesson to all future tyrants." The king gone, the Puritan Parliament abolished the House of Lords, declared the People under God the origin of all just power, and declared England to be a Commonwealth. Confusion followed. They had gone too far too fast.

Oliver Cromwell

Oliver Cromwell hoped for moderation, unity, religious tolerance, but with his Parliament gone mad, it was impossible. He dismissed it. Against his will, he, Oliver Cromwell, had to rule as a tyrant. There was no other way to restore order at home or respect for England abroad. This he accomplished with the aid of his able secretary, the great poet Milton. His government, however, had not been established, nor the King been beheaded by the will of the majority. Besides the Royalists, many others were dissatisfied under the grim supervision of Puritans, who condemned all pleasure as sin. They allowed no Christmas celebration, no Maypole dancing, no card playing, no ale drinking. Ever on the alert, they found reason to remove from his parish a certain clergyman whose name was Washington and whose son John sailed in 1657, taking the famous name to Virginia.

Oliver Cromwell died in 1658. The people, sick of life without any pleasure, soon got their fill of it when they called for another king and got a happy-go-lucky, extravagantly "merry monarch" who thought of nothing much but making love to the ladies— Charles II.

Charles · James · Mary

In May, 1660, on his thirtieth birthday, Charles II reached London. Crowds of cheering people lined the streets to catch a glimpse of their new King. What they saw was a big, swarthy, good-natured young man with a loose red mouth and roving dark eyes. What they also saw was a King who knew nothing about England and cared little. He had been gone since he was nineteen, when his father was beheaded. Since then he had been drifting around the Continent, living partly with his cousin Louis XIV, the King of France, partly with his sister Mary and her husband, William II of Holland—anywhere that he could get money to pay for his kind of pleasure.

Becoming King did not change him. Neither his way of life, nor his need of money, nor the unscrupulous means he used to get his hands on it. He robbed the treasury, cheated the navy and caused a financial panic when Parliament did not grant him enough funds to squander.

Sir William Penn once loaned the King $80,000. After Penn's death, his son William persuaded Charles II to pay off the debt in American land. Penn wished to found a colony for Friends, or Quakers, and proposed to call it Sylvania (woods). The King prefixed Penn, so it became Pennsylvania.

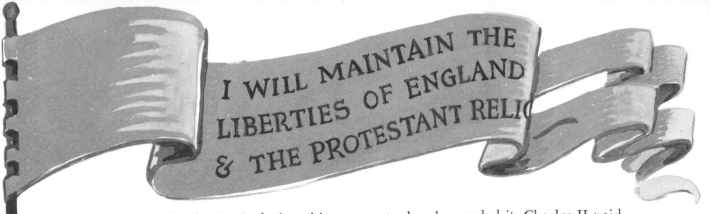

I WILL MAINTAIN THE LIBERTIES OF ENGLAND & THE PROTESTANT RELIC

To Holland, who had given him support when he needed it, Charles II paid his debt in a more characteristic way. After signing a treaty to respect Holland's colony on the Hudson River, he sent a secret expedition to surprise and capture the town of New Amsterdam, which he renamed New York, to honor his brother James, the Duke of York—later James II.

Englishmen make their liberties secure in a
BILL OF RIGHTS

James II became King in 1685, when Charles II died. Charles had no heir. James had a daughter Mary, who was the wife of her cousin, William III of Holland. When, after three years, James was no longer to be endured, Parliament sent to William III, asking him to sail with an army to England and defend his wife's right to the throne. Mary said she wanted to share it with her husband, and rule as William and Mary, which was most pleasing to him.

So William sailed and Uncle James fled. Although the flag on William's ship bore the words: "I will maintain the liberties of England and the Protestant religion," the people of England were taking no more chances with unsigned promises. Before the coronation, Parliament issued a formal list of rights to the people, making it clear that . . .

THE KING HELD HIS OFFICE AND POWER BY THE WILL OF THE PEOPLE.

NO TAXES WERE TO BE PUT UPON THE PEOPLE WITHOUT THEIR CONSENT.

In 1688 this Bill of Rights, signed by William and Mary, became a law.

Like the Magna Carta in 1215, it marks a great birthday of freedom for England. By it, the idea of the divine right of a king to rule without accounting to the people came to an end forever in England.

Louis XIV

Louis XIV of France was the all-powerful King, the absolute ruler, the envy of all other kings of Europe who believed as he did that "kings are gods and bear on their forehead a divine character." He also said, "To rule by work is the true secret of power." And Louis XIV worked at the job of ruling eight hours a day for seventy-two years, from 1643 to 1715. The King worked. His nobles did nothing. They merely revolved around him like planets around the sun. He, their "Sun King," had arranged it that way. Why should he let them be scattered on their various estates where they might become rebellious? No. Let them live near his palace at Versailles, beautiful and new, where he could keep an eye on them. To make them happy, he gave them honorary offices, such as handing him his wig, serving his breakfast, to which large pay and no work were attached.

And they paid no taxes. Taxes were paid by those who worked: the peasants, the merchants and tradesmen, the bourgeoisie. And who dared to complain?

Voltaire did. And he was thrown into prison in 1717 when he was twenty-three for saying what he thought about such injustice. Later the young author took refuge in England for three years.

"In England," he said, "you do not hear of one kind of justice for the higher class of people and another for the lower. An Englishman is not exempt from paying certain taxes just because he is a nobleman. A government like that of ours in France which permits a certain class of men to say, 'Let those who work pay taxes; we should not pay taxes because we do not work,' is no better than a government of Hottentots."

No government was good, by kings or by Parliaments. So said another critical Frenchman, Rousseau. Also, too much civilization was bad. To be free, men should return to the simple life of primitive tribes in the wilderness—for example—the red Indians in America.

Most Frenchmen said nothing. But they did a great deal of thinking, especially after these men, Voltaire and Rousseau, had given words to their thoughts.

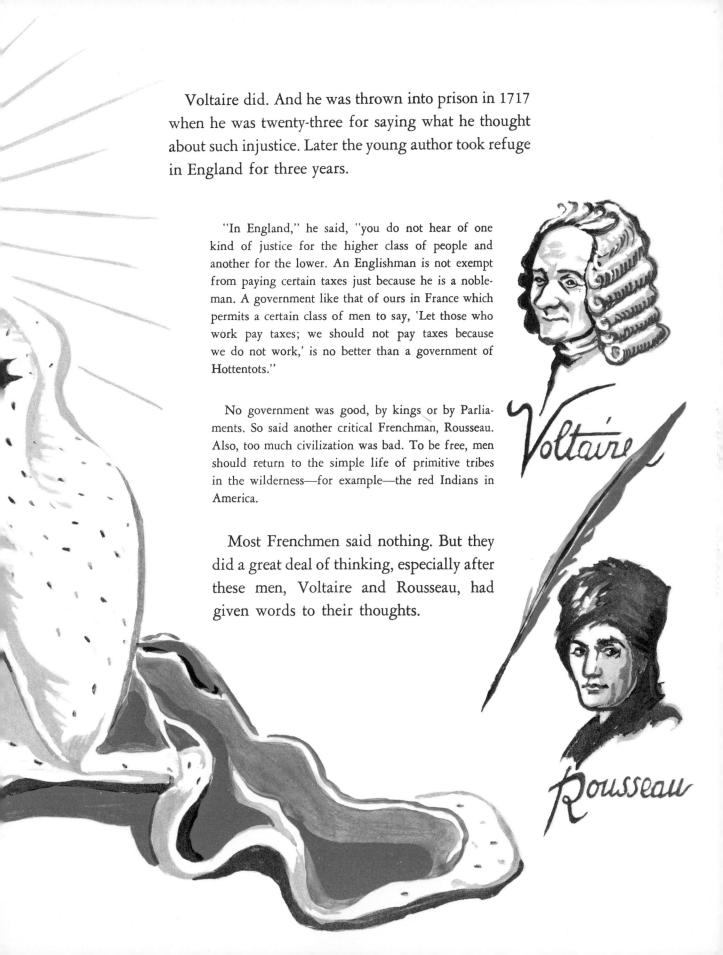

Louisiana, a new colony named for the King, Louis XIV, was now added to New France in America. In 1682 the French explorer La Salle, starting from the Canadian shore of the Great Lakes, sailed down the Mississippi River to the mouth and there, planting the cross and the lilies of France, claimed all the land watered by the great river for his King. A vast territory it was, six times that of France itself. Compared to it, the colonies of England were inconsequential, just a narrow border along the Atlantic Ocean, as yet reaching no farther west than the Allegheny Mountain wall. In their charters, however, each colony was vaguely but handsomely described as reaching from sea to sea. So it was inevitable that, as the French kept building forts closer to the English settlements, there should be disputes over the uncertain borderline. In 1754 the disputes exploded into war, as the English tried to drive the French from a small log fort they had built at the head of the Ohio River. Colonial

fight for land in America.

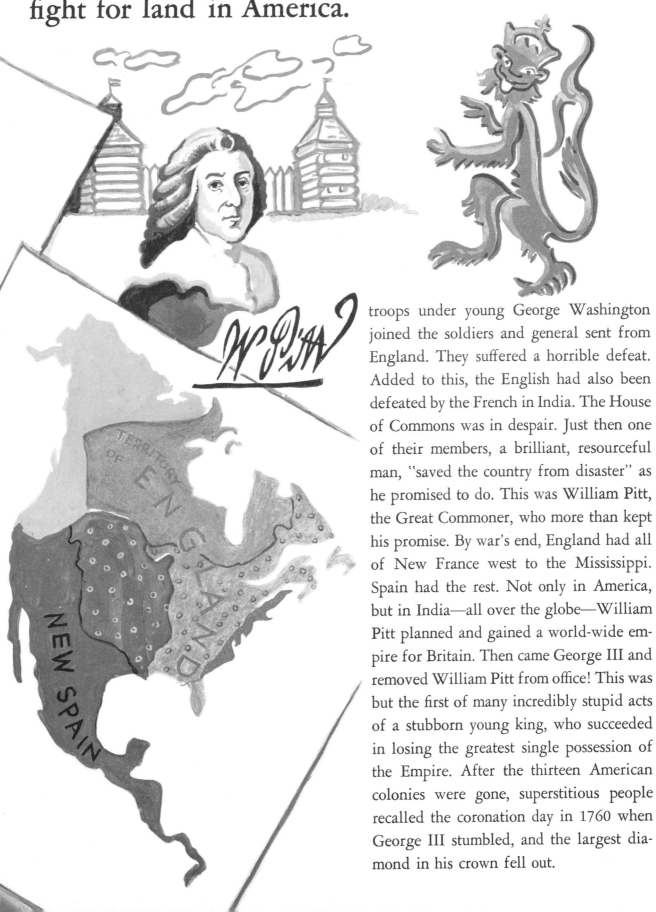

troops under young George Washington joined the soldiers and general sent from England. They suffered a horrible defeat. Added to this, the English had also been defeated by the French in India. The House of Commons was in despair. Just then one of their members, a brilliant, resourceful man, "saved the country from disaster" as he promised to do. This was William Pitt, the Great Commoner, who more than kept his promise. By war's end, England had all of New France west to the Mississippi. Spain had the rest. Not only in America, but in India—all over the globe—William Pitt planned and gained a world-wide empire for Britain. Then came George III and removed William Pitt from office! This was but the first of many incredibly stupid acts of a stubborn young king, who succeeded in losing the greatest single possession of the Empire. After the thirteen American colonies were gone, superstitious people recalled the coronation day in 1760 when George III stumbled, and the largest diamond in his crown fell out.

Americans fight for their rights as Englishmen.

George III was a young man of great self-confidence, patriotic and proud of being the first of three Georges to be born in England.

George I was a German, from Saxony, the land from which the Saxon invaders of England had originally come. He could not speak a word of English. He had no desire to be King of England. So why bother about it? Let the Parliament run the country to suit themselves.

George II was a true German warrior. He loved nothing better than to fight. He was the King who, when war was going badly in America and India, gave William Pitt his "comblete confidentz." He also let Parliament run the government. "In dis country," he said, "the ministers are the king."

George III had other ideas, drilled into him by his mother. "When you get to be king," she told him, "BE King!" That is what he started out to be with utmost self-confidence. First he tried out one Prime Minister after another until he found a "yes" man. Then by bribes at elections, he filled the House of Commons with members who would vote for the laws he wanted passed. Tax laws came first—to pay for the costly wars against the French. In America, he argued, who would benefit most from having the French driven out? The colonists, of course, the English in America. Therefore, let them pay the cost. Just two

LLION! 1775

years after the war was settled, came the Stamp Act, that tax which caused such rebellion as to make William Pitt ask Benjamin Franklin if the Americans actually wished to be independent. That was 1765. For the next ten years Benjamin Franklin was in England, hoping that the trouble between the King and the colonies could be settled peaceably. But before 1775, when he returned home, tea had been dumped in Boston harbor. Boston citizens had been fired upon by British soldiers in what Samuel Adams called a "massacre." And in April, 1775, the first shots had been fired at Lexington and Concord.

In May, Benjamin Franklin landed in Philadelphia and went as a delegate to the Congress meeting in the State House on May 10. George Washington appeared in uniform, prepared for action. At John Adams' suggestion, Washington was appointed to take command of the colonial army outside of Boston. He was there until the following spring.

By that time Thomas Paine, an Englishman, newly arrived in Philadelphia, had written a pamphlet called "Common Sense," and with stirring words roused the people to turn this war of rebellion into a war for independence.

"O ye that love mankind, ye that dare not only to oppose tyranny but the tyrant stand forth. Every spot in the old world is overrun with oppression . . .

The birthday of a new world is at hand!"

In 1776 the United States

Thomas Jefferson had written the words of the Declaration of Independence, and on July 4, seated beside Benjamin Franklin, had heard the final draft of that most important paper read aloud to Congress, voted upon and accepted. Four days later, on July 8, the ringing of the Liberty Bell summoned the people of Philadelphia to hear the Declaration read to them from the wooden platform in the State House square.

Fifty-six men from the thirteen colonies signed the Declaration after it had been copied on parchment, the first and largest signature being that of John Hancock, president of the Congress.

The unanimous Declaration

When in the course of human Events, it becomes necessary for one People to dissolve the Political Bands which have connected them with another, and to assume among the Powers of the Earth, the separate and equal Station to which the Laws of Nature and of Nature's God entitle them, a decent Respect to the Opinions of Mankind requires that they should declare the causes which impel them to the Separation.

7 6

of America was born.

George Washington did not sign the Declaration of Independence, but more than any other man he turned those words written on paper into a reality. On the day that Congress voted for independence, Washington was in New York City with his army, preparing to defend the city. There he received a copy of the Declaration, and on the day after it had been read aloud in Philadelphia, his soldiers heard it read to them by their battalion commanders. These are the words they heard. They mark a climax in the story of Freedom, a story which can never end.

of the thirteen united States of America,

We hold these Truths to be self-evident, that all Men are created equal, that they are endowed by their Creator with certain unalienable Rights, that among these are Life, Liberty, and the Pursuit of Happiness—That to secure these Rights, Governments are instituted among Men, deriving their just Powers from the Consent of the Governed, that whenever any Form of Government becomes destructive of these Ends, it is the Right of the People to alter or to abolish it, and to institute new Government, laying its Foundation on such Principles, and organizing its Powers in such Form, as to them shall seem most likely to effect their Safety and Happiness. Prudence, indeed, will dictate that Governments long established should not be changed for light and transient causes; and accordingly all Experience hath shown, that Mankind are more disposed to suffer, while Evils are sufferable, than to right themselves by abolishing the Forms to which they are accustomed. But when a long Train of Abuses and Usurpations, pursuing invariably the same Object, evinces a Design to reduce them under absolute Despotism, it is their Right, it is their Duty, to throw off such Government, and to provide new Guards for their future Security. Such has been the patient Sufferance of these Colonies; and such is now the Necessity which constrains them to alter their former Systems of Government. The History of the present King of Great-Britain is a History of repeated Injuries and Usurpations, all having in direct Object the Establishment of an absolute Tyranny over these States. To prove this, let Facts be submitted to a candid World.

(Here follows a long list of grievances against the King, "for imposing taxes on us without our consent—depriving us of trial by jury—quartering large bodies of troops among us—taking away our charters—abolishing our most valuable laws, etc.," leading to this conclusion:)

We, therefore, the Representatives of the UNITED STATES OF AMERICA, in GENERAL CONGRESS, Assembled, appealing to the Supreme Judge of the World for the Rectitude of our Intentions, do, in the Name, and by Authority of the good People of these Colonies, solemnly Publish and Declare, That these United Colonies are, and of Right ought to be, FREE AND INDEPENDENT STATES; that they are absolved from all Allegiance to the British Crown, and that all political Connection between them and the State of Great-Britain, is and ought to be totally dissolved; and that as FREE AND INDEPENDENT STATES, they have full Power to levy War, conclude Peace, contract Alliances, establish Commerce, and to do all other Acts and Things which INDEPENDENT STATES may of right do. And for the support of this Declaration, with a firm Reliance on the Protection of divine Providence, we mutually pledge to each other our Lives, our Fortunes, and our sacred Honor.